THEN AND T
GENERAL
MARJORIE REEVE

The Pilgrim Fathers

W. J. C. GILL, B.A., A.K.C.

Illustrated from contemporary sources by

BARBOSA and H. S. WHITEHORNE

LONGMAN

LONGMAN GROUP LIMITED
London

*Associated companies, branches and representatives
throughout the world*

*First published 1964
Sixth impression 1972*

ISBN 0 582 20395 3

FOR GILLIAN

ACKNOWLEDGEMENTS

We are grateful to Cassell & Co. Ltd. and Little, Brown and Co., Publishers for permission to include material from *The Voyage of Mayflower II* by Warwick Charlton, published in the U.S.A. under the title *The Second Mayflower Adventure,* Copyright © 1957, by Little, Brown & Company.

For permission to include drawings based on copyright material we are indebted to the following: Constable & Co., Ltd.—page 9 from Dexter: *The England and Holland of the Pilgrims;* Alfred Knopf Inc.—pages 32/33 37 and 41 from Bradford: *Plymouth Plantation 1620-1647;* the Pilgrim Society, Plymouth, Massachusetts —pages 19 and 65.

*Printed in Hong Kong by
Peninsula Press Ltd*

CONTENTS

TO THE READER

The story that you will read in this book is a true one. Although the events in it took place a long time ago, we know a good deal about them. The reason for this is that some of the people you will meet wrote down the story of what they did. These diaries or journals have survived and I have used them to tell you about them. One day you may want to read more for yourselves. If you do, the best one to get is *Of Plymouth Plantation* by William Bradford. Two others are *A Description of New England* by Captain John Smith and—a long title, this one—*A Relation or Journal of the Beginnings and Proceedings of the English Plantation settled at Plimoth in New England* by G. Mourt. This is usually called *Mourt's Relation* for short.

In the book we are really only concerned with how and why the Pilgrims went to New England and how they settled there. You will find, therefore, that I have not gone beyond their first year there. If you are interested you may like to try to find out for yourselves what happened later.

Thanksgiving

On the morning of the fourth Thursday in November children all over the United States, and particularly in New England, wake up early in great excitement. It is Thanksgiving: a whole holiday from school; a day when uncles and aunts and cousins and grown-up brothers and sisters all come together. It is almost like Christmas. It is a day for going to church in the morning and for sitting down to an enormous lunch of turkey with *cranberry* sauce followed by *pumpkin* pie. It is a day for talking and visiting a ball game and for family parties. It is a day that we do not have in England, although there are many things for which we could give thanks.

To understand why the Americans have this national holiday we have to go back in our imaginations hundreds of years to the early winter of 1621. We must have a picture in our minds of an America largely uninhabited: without its towns and cities; without all the things that we think of as typically American. We have to see a land of forest and *prairie*; a land of Red Indians and buffaloes; a land upon whose eastern coast, dotted here and there, are tiny little settlements of Europeans—English, Dutch, Spanish. In particular we must try to see a bay in the northern parts, where twenty or so wooden cabins stand on the shore, dominated by a platform on a hill upon which are two or three cannon. It is a quiet place. Around it are small cultivated fields, bare now, and, beyond them, the forests stretching away into the distance. If we look carefully we can see a few roughly-dressed men and women moving about among the cabins; there is smoke coming from the home-made chimneys and, despite the loneliness of the place, there is an atmosphere of cheerfulness. It is difficult for us to think how the people there can be cheerful. They are at the beginning of a long, hard winter and their houses do not seem to be very snug and warm. They are on the very edge of the land and the forests look as though they might move forwards and drive these *interlopers* back into the sea.

Yet they are cheerful with reason. They have braved a stormy passage of the Atlantic; they have built their little homes themselves; they have survived one hard winter, although over half their number died; they have ploughed and sown and reaped. Their crops are safely in and they are giving thanks to God for the passing of their first year in the New World. It is both right and fitting that they should thank God, for they have given up their homes and work in England to adventure into this cold and *hostile* world, so that they might practise their religion as they wish without anyone trying to stop them. On this day therefore they rejoice.

Let one of the settlers tell us what they are doing. The speaker is Edward Winslow. He says:

'Our harvest being gotten in, our Governor sent four men on *fowling*, that so we might, after a more special manner, rejoice together after we had gathered the fruit of our labours. They four, in one day, killed as much fowl as, with a little help besides, served the company almost a week. At which time, amongst other recreations, we *exercised* our arms (showed our skill with guns and swords), many of the Indians coming among us, and amongst the rest their greatest king, Massasoit, with some ninety men whom for three days we entertained and feasted. And they went out and killed five deer which they

2

brought to the plantation and bestowed on our Governor and upon the Captain and others.'

We can imagine the scene. The colonists had gone out and laid in plentiful provisions for the feast. They had shot quantities of wild turkeys; they had picked berries to give flavour; they had brought in pumpkins. And then there descended upon them this horde of hungry Indians! Certainly the visitors provided *venison* but they also stayed for three days and ate the settlers out of house and home. But, although they must have worried about how to feed everyone, we can believe that the little band of English folk was pleased to welcome the Indians. It had been an anxious year; they had feared all the time a surprise attack from the Red Indians and had always gone armed. Now it seemed as though they might be able to make friends with these fierce warriors.

This was the first Thanksgiving; these were the first settlers of New England. In the rest of this book we shall be finding out more about them; why they came to America, where they came from, how they crossed the broad Atlantic and how they survived this, their first year.

The Pilgrimage Begins

The story really begins in the little village of Scrooby in Nottinghamshire where a group of people who lived in this neighbourhood decided to leave their homes and go to live first in Holland and then in America. Why did they do this? We must first find out what led them to take this very daring decision.

You probably know already quite a lot about Henry VIII, Martin Luther and the events that led some countries and some people to decide that they could no longer agree with all the teachings of the Roman Catholic Church and that they would like a different type of church. This movement was called the 'Reformation' and the new churches the 'Reformed' churches. You will notice that I said 'churches'. I put it in the plural because, although the reformers disagreed with the Roman Catholics, they also disagreed with each other. Many of the English, and particularly Queen Elizabeth and James I, wanted to keep the bishops and many of the ceremonies of the Catholics, while having the reform ideas taught. Others wanted quite a new church, governed by a meeting called a *synod* and by leaders called *elders*. Others still wanted a whole series of independent churches that were quite separate from each other and decided all things for themselves. We can pick three examples to make this clearer:

1. The Church of England. This kept *Archbishops*, *Bishops* and most other Catholic ranks; its priests wore *vestments*; it used a *prayer-book*.

2. *Presbyterians.* This group believed in a simple form of service but all the churches were governed by a central council—the synod we mentioned above.

3. Congregationalists. These people believed each church should be quite independent. Services were very simple, and there were no vestments or special ceremonies. Each church looked after its own affairs and picked (or elected) its own *pastor*.

You will say, quite possibly, that there is nothing very remarkable about this. For us, living in the twentieth century, when we can attend any church we wish, or none at all, it is indeed nothing to wonder at. For the sixteenth

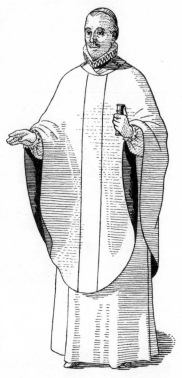

An Anglican priest wearing vestments—notably alb and chasuble

and seventeenth centuries, however, it was quite different. For one thing, each church believed that it was the only true church and that every other was both wrong and evil. They were quite prepared to fight for their own faith and also fight to force everyone to agree with them. For another, the rulers of the country were accustomed to having everyone agree with them. It was quite unthinkable for a sixteenth-century king or queen to allow people to make up their own minds on religion or anything else. Anyone who disagreed with the ruler was a *traitor* and was punished accordingly.

5

A Presbyterian minister wearing his black gown

When the *Reformation* reached England many people hoped to have their own kind of church. Books were written defending one kind of faith; others were written *denouncing* the first books and a war of words developed. English rulers, and particularly Elizabeth, tried to bring order out of the *chaos* by issuing orders about religion. So the struggle began between the government and those of the people who thought their ideas were better. Such people were those of Scrooby.

Let us look a little more closely at the attempts by the English government to organize a church and try to see why it thought it was acting rightly.

When Elizabeth became Queen she found England quite split between the Roman Catholics and the Reformers. There seemed to be real danger of a *civil war*. Elizabeth wanted her country to be united and also wanted to be secure on the throne. With this in mind she created the Church of England. As we have noticed, this Church appeared more or less Roman Catholic in its services but the teaching was that of the Reformers. Her idea was to make the Church acceptable to most Roman Catholics and most Reformers. She wanted them all to feel at home there. In this she was remarkably successful, though of course some Roman Catholics and some Reformers would not accept it. Those Reformers who did accept the Church were hoping that they would be able to change it more to their way. They objected especially to all those things which reminded them of the Catholic Church such as *surplices*, vestments, bowing to the *altar*, *crucifixes* and so on. It was many years before they decided, sadly, that the job of trying to change things was hopeless and left the Church.

Meanwhile the Queen was becoming more and more angry with those who criticized her Church. She called them traitors, arrested them, imprisoned them and even hanged them. Those who suffered included both Reformers and Catholics.

In 1603 Queen Elizabeth died. She was succeeded by James VI of Scotland. The main church in Scotland was the Presbyterian Church, so the English Reformers hoped that James would help them to put the Church of England right. Unfortunately for them James had disliked the Scottish Reformers intensely. They had, he thought, no respect for him as King. On one occasion indeed, in a sermon preached before him, the minister had referred to him as 'God's silly *vassal*'. He thought the English bishops would be much more respectful and, furthermore, he believed that it was his right, as King, to be the head of the Church. Quite early, therefore, he announced his determination to force the Reformers to obey the rules of the *Anglican* Church. All over the land the lives of these earnest and sincere men and women became harder and harder: some gave in; others suffered imprisonment and others still decided to leave England and seek a refuge in Holland where they were sure they could find the freedom they desired. It is the story of one such group that we are telling.

Scrooby

Towards the end of the sixteenth century there lived in the manor-house of Scrooby one William Brewster. He did not own the house but was there as a kind of agent for the real owner. He was, in addition, the postmaster. He was not the kind of postmaster that we have today for, in those days, there were no post offices or postage stamps or telegrams. He was rather the man who was responsible for the sending on of government *despatches*. There were many such places in England, usually separated by about twenty miles. The government letters would go from one stage-post to the next. He also had to keep horses and rooms for government officials and important travellers. They would stay the night with him, obtain fresh horses and travel on to the next stage. It was quite well-paid work, so, with this and his agency, William Brewster was probably the most important man in the village.

Although he had a lot to do, Brewster, who was deeply religious, still found time to join the Reformers and did much to spread their ideas. Gradually, quite a group of them came together there and met every Sunday in the manor-house. There were two or three Anglican priests around Scrooby who were also Reformers and they acted as ministers. The most important were Richard Clifton, John Smyth and, later, John Robinson.

8

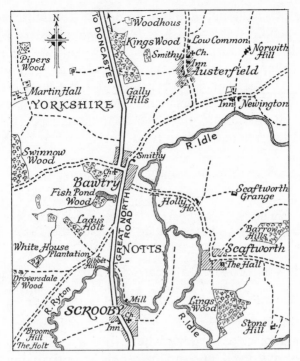

The area from which the Pilgrims came

I don't think you would have greatly enjoyed one of these 'reformed' services. Here is a description of one:

'We begin with prayer; afterwards we read one or two chapters of the Bible, give the sense thereof and discuss it. The first speaker then announces a text and preaches on it for about an hour. Then the second speaker talks on the same text for the same length of time and after him the third, fourth and maybe the fifth.'

This morning *exercise* began at eight o'clock and continued till about twelve; in the afternoon there was a similar service from two p.m. until five or six. Then there was a meeting to deal with church business.

9

We can imagine, as the government net tightened and more people were punished for not going to the parish church, that the time for church business was more and more taken up by discussion as to what they should do: should they stay or should they try to leave England? And then, when they had decided to go, there must have been much discussion of how they should escape, for they would be arrested if they tried to *emigrate* in the normal way.

In 1608 we find in a diary the following entry:

> 'Seeing themselves thus *molested*, and that there was no hope of their continuance there, by a joynte consente they resolved to go into ye *Low Countries*, wher they heard was freedome of Religion for all men.'

This was probably a great adventure for the children but it was a sad and anxious moment for the grown-ups. They had to face giving up all their possessions, their houses and farms, or their jobs; they would have to leave the small piece of England where they and their ancestors had always lived and go to a new country where, not knowing the language, they would have to find work and shelter. It was a bitter prospect but they were prepared to do it for the sake of their religion.

The Journey to Holland

One group from Scrooby came to an arrangement with the captain of a small ship. He agreed to pick them up from a lonely part of the coast near Boston in Lincolnshire. Sadly they left their homes and, with their few possessions, travelled across country to the appointed place. There, on the shore, they waited but the ship did not come. They were hungry, they were weary and they were frightened. They could not give up and go home, because they no longer had homes. At last, however, after darkness had fallen, the ship came. Quickly, and with tremendous relief, they climbed aboard. The captain, however, had betrayed them. The King's officers were waiting for them on the ship and

'tooke them and put them into open boats and *rifled* and *ransacked* them and then carried them back into ye towne and made them a spectacle and wonder to ye *multitude*.'

Not only, then, was their voyage stopped but, also, they lost all their possessions; they were taken before the magistrates and they were put in prison. Most of them were released after a month but seven who were regarded as leaders, and among whom was Brewster, were held for a longer period.

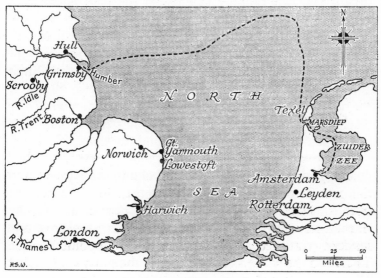

The escape-route to Holland

In the spring of 1608 another group tried to escape. Quite possibly many of them were from the first party and were still determined to *emigrate*. This time the prospects were better. A Dutch shipowner, whom they had met in the port of Hull, had agreed to help them and to see them safely to Holland. The plan was that he should pick up the men from a lonely part of the shore between Grimsby and Hull. They were going to walk there from Scrooby. The women and children were to travel by a small boat along the coast, after floating down the Idle to the Trent, and down the Trent to the Humber, and so round to the point of departure. The women had a voyage of between sixty and seventy miles and the men a cross-country trudge of between forty and fifty.

The small ship carrying the women and children reached the rendezvous a day early. The weather, unfortunately, was rough and most of the passengers were wretchedly seasick. Because they begged very hard, the master put in to a small inlet, so that they might rest in calm water. Even more unfortunately, when the tide went out they became stuck on a mud-bank, just as the Dutch ship appeared. While the little ship waited for high water, the boats of the big ship began ferrying the men off the beach. They had made one trip when the captain saw cavalry and foot-soldiers approaching the shore. They had been betrayed again. The Dutchman at once weighed anchor and sailed away leaving behind the women and children, who were still aground on the mud, and the rest of the men on the shore. The wretched men who had reached the ship could only watch while their wives and children were seized by the soldiers. The remaining men ran away as they felt they could be of more use free than in jail.

When the women and children were arrested they were

taken from one place to another, mainly because no one knew what to do with them. They had no homes to go to and there was no suitable jail for them. They were finally released and were at last able to make their way to Holland to rejoin their husbands and fathers.

Meanwhile the few who had boarded the ship had not had an easy time. The actual distance they had to travel was only about 150 miles, but it was rather a difficult voyage at the Dutch side, as the ship had to sail along the coast skirting the sand-banks and then enter the narrow opening of the *Marsdiep* which led into the *Zuider Zee* and the channels to Amsterdam. Even in fair weather this trip needed a skilled captain; the Pilgrims, for such we may call them now, ran into a fierce storm. The ship was forced north nearly as far as Norway and they spent seven days with no sight of sun, moon or stars. It took them fourteen days to cross the North Sea and several times they were in danger of sinking. The passengers, *fervent* Christians as they were, never gave up hope and prayed unceasingly,

'even when ye water ran into their mouthes and ears and the *mariners* cried out, "We sinke, we sinke".'

The Pilgrims in Holland

After the joyous reunion of families in Holland the Pilgrims began to make plans. They made their homes first in Amsterdam. This was the biggest town in Holland and was a large trading centre and a flourishing port. The population was growing rapidly and there was a great housing shortage. Many had to camp in temporary shelters outside the city walls while new streets were being laid out and new houses erected.

The Pilgrims stayed in Amsterdam for about twelve months. Perhaps they found the town too big after their country life in Scrooby; perhaps they feared they would be lost in the bustling population; perhaps they did not get on too well with the English already there. Whatever the reason, they decided to move as a body to the ancient university town of Leyden. Here they hoped to find homes and work and settle down to live out their peaceful and God-fearing lives. They did not mind what work they did—and indeed the list of jobs they undertook is most impressive. Here are a few:

Baize weaver	Glove maker
Baker	Leather dresser
Brewer's man	Lock maker
Cabinet maker	Looking-glass maker
Candle maker	Printer
Cloth *draper*	Smith
Cloth weaver	Tobacco-pipe maker
Cobbler	

and many more to a total of nearly sixty.

They worked hard but they found it very difficult to make any kind of a living. There were many deaths in the years in Leyden, particularly of children, probably because of the very hard life. Nevertheless, they had achieved something. They were respected citizens of the town, they had their own church and their own beloved pastor, John Robinson. Yet they were uneasy. They were not very worried about the hard work: they worried because the adults were getting older and their children were growing up like little Dutch boys and girls, speaking the Dutch language. They feared that, in twenty years' time, the little English group would be lost in the Dutch nation. Strange as it may seem, although they had more or less been driven out of England, they remained intensely *patriotic*. They could not bring themselves to give up their religious ideas, yet they wished to remain English. Many schemes were discussed but the only possible

North America showing Virginia and Cape Cod

solution seemed to be that they should uproot themselves once more and move to an English colony—probably America.

The American Plan

When they had fixed on America they began to discuss which part they should aim for—should they go south to Guiana or farther north to Virginia which, as you can see from the map, was much bigger than it is today? Further, they had to find someone who would be prepared to give them enough money for this venture.

Finally they decided to go to Virginia and some of the leading members of the community opened discussions

15

with the merchants of the Virginia Company. The bargaining was long and hard. They had to agree to very stiff terms with the company as to how they would repay the loan of money they received.

At last, in 1620, all was done. The King's approval had been secured, two ships, the SPEEDWELL and the MAYFLOWER had been chartered, cargoes and provisions obtained and they now had, once more, to leave familiar surroundings and friends. An advance party was to go first to set up the Colony. It was probably on Friday, 31 July, that the *emigrants* left Leyden for Delftshaven. They travelled by canal through the flat, green fields that they knew so well. At Delftshaven they boarded the SPEEDWELL and, after grief-stricken farewells, sailed on 1 August for England. They could return, though they had fled the country, because King James had agreed to their plan to go to America.

This is how Bradford, one of the travellers, describes the parting in his journal:

'The next day, the wind being faire, they went aborde . . . when truly *doulfull* was the sight of that sad and mournful gathering. But the tide calling them away, their *revered* pastor, falling down on his knees, commended them to the Lorde and his blessing. Then they tooke their leaves one of another; which proved to be the last leave to many of them.'

Arriving in Southampton they found their other ship, the MAYFLOWER, waiting for them. There was a period of tremendous activity to get everything ready, a sale of some of the cargo to pay last minute bills and then, on 5 August, they set sail,

'scarce having any butter, no oyle, not a sole to mend a shoe nor every man a sword to his side, wanting many musketts and much armour.'

The reason why they started out so short of things was that their money had given out.

You will probably be wondering about the MAYFLOWER and what life was like aboard. In the next chapter I will tell you something about the ships of the early seventeenth century in general and, in particular, about the MAY-FLOWER.

The 'Mayflower' and Ships in the Seventeenth Century

'Her *burden* was about nine score'

It is always interesting to take the name of a person or a place or, as in this case, a ship, and try to find out all possible details. It is never easy to be certain that the particular facts you find are correct because, unfortunately, people and ships often have very common names and places sometimes change theirs. Because of this you would have to say 'Probably' or 'I think' rather frequently. This has been so in all the attempts made to describe the MAYFLOWER. Between 1550 and 1700 there were about forty ships with this name. We can, luckily, forget about a lot of them because Governor Bradford of New England mentioned in his Journal that the ship was about 'nine score burden'. This almost certainly means that it was about 180 tons. We can, therefore, cross out all those 'MAYFLOWERS' that were much smaller or much larger. We know, too, from the Journal that the *shallop*, a boat that could carry twenty-five people under sail, was stowed '*betwixt* the decks'. This rules out those remaining ships that did not have two decks. Finally, we know that the captain's name was Christopher Jones and that, in 1620, she was a fairly old ship. Captain John Smith, who was responsible for settling Virginia, described her as 'a leaking, unwholesome ship', and we know, too, that, during the voyage, one of the beams was '*bowed* and cracked'.

18

A reconstructed model of the 'Mayflower'

We are not sure about MAYFLOWER's early career but it is fairly certain that she had spent many years trading with various European ports and there is, too, a very attractive theory, that has some evidence to support it, that the MAYFLOWER of the Pilgrims and a certain 'Mayflower' that fought against the Spanish Armada were one and the same ship.

If we put all our facts together we can picture a fairly old ship, about 180 tons, with two decks. From this, experts have been able to create what must be a fairly accurate description of what the MAYFLOWER must have looked like. They say that such a ship would be about ninety feet long and twenty-five feet wide. It would have three masts, *fore*, *main* and *mizzen*, and a *sprit-sail*, a *fore-sail*, a *fore-topsail*, a *mainsail* and a *main-topsail*. Above you see a drawing of a model of the MAYFLOWER. This model is now in the Hall of the Pilgrim Society at Plymouth, Massachusetts.

Quite clearly the MAYFLOWER was just an ordinary merchant ship of the late sixteenth and early seventeenth centuries. With the knowledge that we have of these ships and life in them we can reconstruct, with some accuracy, the actual ship and life aboard her.

Drawing the plans of a ship

On the facing page are two drawings of such a typical ship.

One, as you can see, is cut across; the other is cut lengthways. It had a rather high front, or bow, with a solid piece of timber, shaped like a beak, projecting. This 'beak' was designed to take the first shock of the waves and, also, to secure the *bowsprit* firmly. In the middle the ship was quite low and then, at the back, it rose again. These high places at the bow and stern were called 'castles'. At one time they

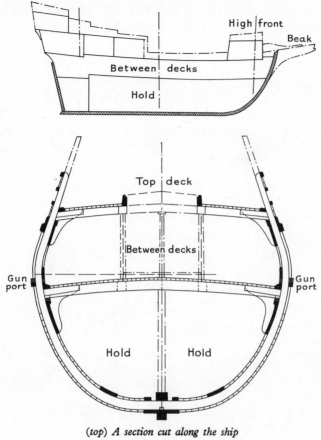

(top) *A section cut along the ship*
(foot) *A section cut across the ship*

were the places from which the ship was defended, or from which attacks were launched on other ships. We still use this word front or 'fore' castle in our modern word 'fo'c'sle', meaning the front of the ship.

Having got an idea what the shape of the vessel is, let us have a walk around it. You will have to bend your heads when we go below deck or you will get a nasty bump as there will never be more than five feet between the floor and the deck above. As we move along, keep an eye on the plan on page 21.

Let us start on the lower deck at the bow. The first thing we can see is a large wooden box stretching from side to side just under the *ports* for the anchor chains. This is called a 'manger' and its purpose is to catch the water which splashes through these ports and which would otherwise run down the deck. Just *aft* of the manger is an enormous wooden pole. This is the *foremast*; it stretches away above us through the upper deck. If we stand by this mast and look towards the *stern* it seems that we are looking down a long tunnel about five feet high and sixty feet long. When we venture down this dark passage about half-way along we come upon an even larger wooden pole: this is the *mainmast* and by it is a *hatchway* into the hold below. This is where the cargo is kept: where all the goods that the Pilgrims were taking to found the colony were stowed.

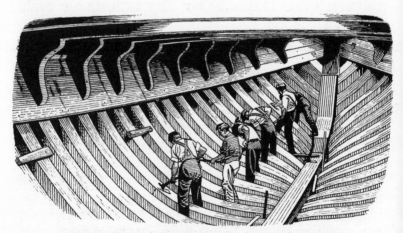

Building ' Mayflower II'—the use of the adze in shaping timber

We won't go down there because it is even darker; there will be rats and, further, it smells very badly. These wooden ships always took in a certain amount of water and, although normally it was not enough to be dangerous, it was rarely pumped dry and, as you know, *stagnant* water soon begins to be very foul.

Continuing towards the stern we see the *mizzen-mast* and also notice that there is a step down in the deck. Below this part of the deck there is a very strongly made compartment in which the gunpowder is stored. This powder is for the guns on board. Two we can see at the stern pointing to the rear and two, or maybe more, we passed walking along the deck. You may wonder why a merchantman should carry guns. There are two reasons for this. One was that, in time of war, merchantmen became warships as they were very similar in construction. The other was that, in these centuries, all the seas were *infested* with pirates. Ships had to be prepared to defend themselves. The drawings below and on page 24 show the kind of cannon that were used. They were not very accurate nor could they fire a long way.

Naval battles were fought at close quarters. The first gun, the *demi-cannon*, was ten feet long and 6·5 inch *calibre*, the others were smaller. The *culverins* fired

Demi-cannon

Culverin

cannon-balls 5·5 inches in diameter or slightly less; *demi-culverins* 4·5 inch, *sakers* 3·5 inch and the smallest, the *minion*, 3·25 inch. In front of each gun was a removable shutter called a gun-port. When the gun was to be fired this port was opened and the gun run forward until the *muzzle* protruded. You can imagine what it must have been like between decks when the guns were fired. The noise must have been tremendous and great clouds of smoke would soon fill the confined space.

In the stern, too, there is the *tiller* handle. Clearly the helmsman would not see very much if he stood down here

Saker

so the control of the tiller is taken up to the top-deck by a device called a whipstaff.

In this dark, confined and unpleasant place most of the Pilgrims and the crew, over a hundred people, would sleep, eat and generally live for some eight weeks. In addition there was also kept here the precious shallop.

Someone described this uncomfortable temporary home in the style of a recipe book:

'Take the ship, add one hundred assorted Pilgrims and a crew of twenty-five; place in the hold all necessary goods for founding a colony; clutter up the space between the decks with a shallop; add cold weather, cold water dripping everywhere through leaking decks and toss liberally around the North Atlantic for two months.'

24

When we climb up through the hatchway we find ourselves in the *steerage*. This is where the helmsman stands. In front of him is the *binnacle*. This is a wooden chest in which are the steering *compass* to give the helmsman his course, *sand-glasses* for telling the passage of time and candles so that he can see the compass at night. This box is fastened to the deck directly in front of the steering. position. As you can see in the drawing the front panel is removable. It is interesting

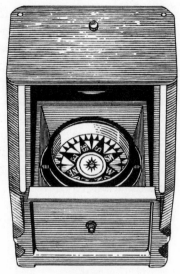

A binnacle

to note that the box is entirely fastened with wooden nails so that no iron is near enough to affect the compass needle.

Behind the steerage is the great cabin. This is, perhaps, the only comfortable and roomy part of the ship. To add to its attraction there are windows overlooking the stern. Here the master and, possibly, important passengers live. Probably the leaders of the Pilgrims travelled in it.

Forward of the steerage is the usual clutter of the deck, masts, ropes, hatchway covers and, possibly, more guns.

The ship is small, cramped and extremely uncomfortable. In good weather it is, perhaps, enjoyable for a time to travel on her; in bad weather, shut up below decks, it must be frightful.

Finding their way

We know that, when the Pilgrims crossed the Atlantic, they made their *landfall* much farther north than they had intended. The amazing thing, when you think about their knowledge of navigation and the instruments they used, is that the sailors ever reached a particular place at all. What did the master have to help him find his way? He had to know where he was, which direction he was travelling in and how fast he was moving. He had also, as he neared land, to be able to find out how deep the water was and how the tides were. It was reasonably easy to know his direction; the compass told him that, but to find out his position at any particular time was a different and more difficult matter.

To help him in this he had an *astrolabe*, a cross-staff or a back-staff. This is what the astrolabe looked like:

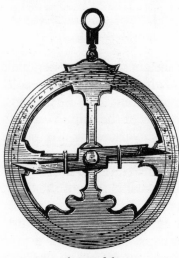

An astrolabe

Each of these was to tell the master the angle between the sun, the ship and the sea. When the master had the size of the angle he then turned to his books. Here he had tables. He looked at the date, the size of the angle and then he could look across the tables and find his *latitude*, that is, how far north or south he was. He could then draw a line across the chart.

He needed, too, to know how far he had travelled westwards. For this he needed to know the speed of the ship. He could then measure the distance he had travelled in, say, the past twenty-four hours and draw a line north to south. This gave him his position where the lines crossed. To get this speed he used the *log and line*. The log was usually a thin board of beechwood about twelve inches high and six inches wide with a strip of lead on the lower edge. This made it float upright in the water. Attached to the log was a long line with knots in it every forty-two feet (every seven fathoms). The method was to put the log in the water. Then, as the ship moved away from it, the line ran out. Over a certain length of time, timed by a sand-glass, a check was made to see how much line had run out. This told the master how far the ship had gone in this length of time. Let us take an example; if in a minute fourteen *fathoms* of line run out that means that the ship has travelled fourteen fathoms—or 84 feet in one minute. So, in one hour it would travel 84×60 feet which is 5,040 feet or 1,680 yards or nearly one mile. Here is a description from an instruction book for the sailors of the time:

A sand-glass

'One stands by with a minute glass whilst another, out of the gallery lets fall the log; just as the log falls into the water, the other turns the glass and just when the glass is even out he cries stop; then he stops and reckons how many fathoms are run out.'

This was a very rough and ready way of deciding speed, for it took no account of currents or tides. With such clumsy and inaccurate instruments, no wonder mistakes about the ship's position were often made.

We may think that travelling in such conditions was both dangerous and difficult. We can look upon the sailors and Pilgrims with even more admiration as we follow them on their toilsome way. But this was recognized at the time. No one looked upon an ocean voyage lightly or tried to make out the sailor's profession to be an easy one. To quote Captain John Smith again:

> 'Men of all other professions in lightning, thunder, storms and tempests may shelter themselves in dry houses by good fires, whereas those are the very times that seamen must stand to their *tacklings* . . . in foule weather the labour, *hazard*, wet and cold are so incredible I cannot express it.'

At last, however, if good fortune has prevailed, the voyage is over. We can see the ship bearing into the land

under topsails with a *leadsman* in the *chains* and the *bosun* and his party forward preparing to let go the anchor. As the ship moves on and is brought round head to wind we hear the splash of her anchor. The dangers and hardships are, now, for the time being forgotten.

If the captain has been a wise man, the crew and passengers will be in good health, for he will have checked personally the buying of the food and will have also provided extra delicacies. He will have bought brandy, currants, sugar, oil, *bitters*, lemons, biscuits, oatmeal and bacon. These extras will have been issued whenever a

A leadsman measuring the depth of the water

28

man was ill, or after a storm when all are wet through. For
this he will have been blessed by his men for at sea

'there is neither ale-house, taverne nor Inne to burne a *faggot* in,
neither grocer, poulterer, *apothecary* nor butcher's shop where men
may buy *liquor*, *victuals* and warmth after a night of storm.'

We must now see if the Pilgrims on the MAYFLOWER
were fortunate enough to have a good voyage.

The Voyage

'All things now being ready . . . the company was called together . . . which being done they set sail on the fifth of August.'

So writes Governor Bradford as, at last, after overcoming all their difficulties, the Pilgrims left the shores of England. For those who were in the SPEEDWELL, however, it was a short voyage. They had not gone very far from Plymouth when Master Reynolds, the Captain of the SPEEDWELL, reported that his ship was leaking so much that he dare go no farther. He consulted Master Jones, Captain of the MAYFLOWER, and they agreed that both ships should put in to Dartmouth for the necessary repairs. This was done 'to the great *charge*' of the Pilgrims, and they sailed on. They had not gone three hundred miles beyond Land's End before the Captain of the SPEEDWELL was again reporting that his ship was leaking and that, if he did not turn back, it would sink. So once more back into port they went. This time the leaders decided that it was a waste of time and money to try to make the SPEEDWELL seaworthy. Actually the master and men of the SPEEDWELL did not want to go to America. They had tricked the Pilgrims by putting into the ship a mainmast that was too high for the size of the ship and carried too many sails. This strained the ship, forced the *seams* open and thus made the ship leak. Later, when a proper mast was put in, the SPEEDWELL was perfectly seaworthy. The Pilgrims, therefore, packed themselves a little more tightly in the MAYFLOWER and

30

took on board as many of the passengers of the SPEEDWELL as they could manage.

On 6 September, with a valuable month wasted, the MAYFLOWER and her passengers finally set sail. At first they had a fair wind and bowled along merrily. Even this, however, made many people seasick. This illness can be very distressing and the Pilgrims were not helped by the jeers and guffaws of the crew who thought it very funny. In particular, one young man seemed to make it his business to be unpleasant to those who were ill. He told them that they would probably die and that he would have much pleasure in helping to put their bodies over the side. Oddly enough all the Pilgrims recovered but the young man fell ill and died. This was regarded by everyone on board as a judgement from heaven.

Soon, unfortunately, the fair wind was replaced by the usual North Atlantic autumnal gales. There were fierce storms in which the little ship was tossed about like a cockleshell; her sails were torn and her timbers creaked and groaned in protest. During one particularly violent period one of the main beams cracked and came out of place. The crew was sure that the MAYFLOWER was about to break up. The Pilgrims, however, were made of sterner stuff. They had to be, considering the kind of life they were going to lead. They were capable, practical men too, for they saw how the damage might be repaired. One of them had what he called a 'great screw'. It must have been something like a motor-car jack which, as you know, is put under a car and turned so that the car is raised off the floor. He brought this and put it under the beam, forced it back into place and held it there until a stout post could be wedged beneath it.

During another storm the ship made no progress westwards for days. The passengers were all below decks as it

Map showing the position of the colony

was unsafe to venture out because of the huge waves. One young man, however, John Howland by name, climbed out on deck. I should think he was in need of fresh air, as it must have been frightful below decks with people crammed into their tiny quarters in complete darkness and thinking every moment would be their last. The journal of the voyage tells us that no sooner had he stepped out on deck than a huge wave broke over the ship and hurled him over

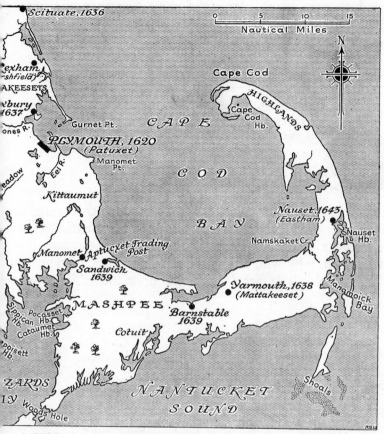

the side. By the greatest good fortune he managed to catch hold of a rope that was trailing over the side and to hang on to it, even though he went far below the surface of the sea. At considerable risk to themselves the crew managed to haul him back: I should not think that he was very popular.

Two months of experiences like this must have made the sight of land almost unbelievable to the passengers and crew. The first landfall was at Cape Cod (look for it on the map), much farther north than they had intended. They tried to turn south along the coast but soon ran into dangerous waters and, rather than risk the ship running on to a sandbank, they decided to turn back and anchored by Cape Cod in Cape Harbour on 11 November. Once they were safely there they thanked God for their safe arrival:

'Being thus arrived in a good harbour, and brought safe to land, they fell upon their knees and blessed the God of Heaven who had brought them over the vast and furious ocean.'

Finding the Settlement

The Pilgrims had their dreadful voyage behind them but facing them were dangers and hardships that were, if anything, even greater. They had to make themselves a home in a wilderness that, so far as they knew, was inhabited only by wild animals and wilder men. The bitter winter of North America was almost upon them. There was

A shallop—the kind of small boat used by the Pilgrims

34

no one to welcome them; no one to help them; nowhere to live. Most people would have given way to despair and, probably, many of the colonists did but there were hardy souls among them with an unshakeable faith in God's ability to help them and in their own skill and endurance.

It was essential that they should find homes ashore as soon as possible. They were living on the MAYFLOWER in great discomfort and everyone wanted to get on to dry land quickly. The leaders, therefore, decided to send out exploring parties to find a suitable site for the settlement. They had brought a boat with them—they called it a 'shallop'. This was a small boat that could be rowed or sailed along the shore and up rivers and this was to be the means of finding a home quickly. The boat had been packed in sections in the lower deck of the MAYFLOWER. You can imagine their dismay when, on getting out the sections to assemble, they found that the battering the MAYFLOWER had received had damaged their boat too. The ship's carpenter told them it would take some days to repair it, and so the leaders decided to send a party ashore on foot in order not to waste too much time.

The First Party

Sixteen of the sturdiest men were to be the first to brave the unknown dangers. They were led by Captain Miles Standish. He was a man of about thirty-six and was a skilled and experienced soldier. The ship's boat put them ashore. You can imagine the scene. The small body of men clad in worn clothes with a coat of mail on top, carrying *muskets* and *cutlasses*, facing the huge and unknown land. They knew that the position was desperate, and so off they marched, stern and resolute. After they had covered about a mile along the shore they saw, in the distance, a group of

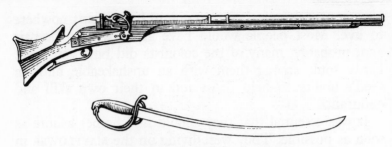
Seventeenth century musket and cutlass

five or six men with a dog. They were the natives whom we today call Red Indians. As soon as the Indians saw them they ran away into the woods with the Pilgrims in hot pursuit. They wanted to try to ask them questions about food and water but they could not catch them. By the time they had given up the chase night was falling and so they decided to camp. It must have been a strange sensation for them—alone in a strange land and expecting an attack by a horde of savages. The night passed quite uneventfully, however, and next day they continued their march. After a time they came upon a patch of cleared ground which seemed to have been an Indian settlement. There were graves, the remains of huts and some curious mounds of loose earth. They dug into these piles of soil with their bare hands and were overjoyed to find that they had come upon a store of *corn*. In the mounds were baskets of corn. This was to be a veritable godsend as, later, such finds gave them seed for their fields. They were very careful to pay back the corn they had borrowed in this way when they obtained their first harvest.

Near by there was a bay that looked as though it might be suitable for ships. This was important, as they needed a safe harbour for the MAYFLOWER and also, later, when the settlement had been established, they would need a safe

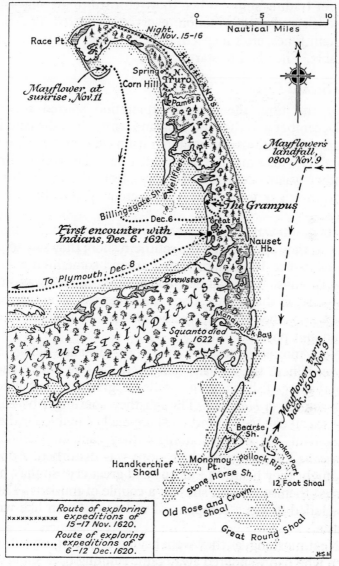

Final stages of the voyage and early explorations

37

bay for trading ships. When they returned to the ship and passed on the information everyone cheered up, but Captain Jones, after inspecting the bay, said that it was not suitable. They had to start again.

The Second Party

By the time the second exploration started it was 11 December and the New England winter had the land in its grip. Conditions on the ship must have been almost unbearable. This time they were able to use the shallop. The weather was so cold that the spray from the waves froze on to their clothes so that 'they were as if they had been *glazed*'.

Their aim was to explore the bay of Cape Cod. As night fell and they approached the southern shore they saw some ten or twelve Indians crowding around something at the water's edge. They landed about three miles away and camped for the night. They were fearful of a surprise attack, so they fenced themselves in as well as they could and posted sentries.

Next morning they marched some distance along the shore. Where the Indians had been the day before they found a large fish which they called a 'grampus' but which was actually a *blackfish*. Though they continued by land and sea all day they found nowhere really suitable for their settlement. Once again at night they camped behind a *barricade* but this time their sleep was disturbed. About midnight they heard 'a hideous and great cry' so they bestirred themselves and shot off a couple of muskets. They concluded it was a company of wolves or 'such like wild beasts'.

Next morning, as they were having breakfast, one of the men who had wandered away came running back shouting 'Indians!' To prove the truth of his warning, arrows came flying amongst them. The Pilgrims put on their armour in frantic haste, seized their muskets, returned the fire and drove off the attackers. This is not quite true. One of the Indians,

> 'a lusty man stood behind a tree within half a musket shot and let his arrows fly at them; he was seen to shoot three arrows which were all avoided. He [with]stood three shots of a musket till one, taking full aim at him, made the bark, or splinters of the tree, fly about his ears, after which he gave an extraordinary shriek and went away.'

Although they had beaten off this attack it must have left the Pilgrims very worried. It seemed clear that the Indians were going to be a danger and that the settlement would always have to be on guard. After the battle they returned to the shallop. They were beset by a great storm; the rudder and the mast broke but they did manage to sail safely through many dangers into another bay. That night they rested safely on an island. Next day, we are told, was fair and sunny. They were able to dry their things and, as it was the Sabbath, give God thanks for their deliverance from many perils.

On Monday they explored the bay. They found it deep enough for big ships; the surrounding land had many streams of fresh water and the ground seemed suitable for farming.

> 'So they returned to their ship again with this news to the rest of their people which did much to comfort their hearts.'

On 15 December the MAYFLOWER sailed for the new home. On the sixteenth they 'resolved where to pitch their dwellings, and on the twenty-fifth day began to erect the first house for common use to receive them and their goods'.

So began the settlement of New Plymouth.

The First Year

We left the explorers, at the end of the last chapter, believing that, at last, they had found the ideal place for a settlement. In great haste, you remember, they had made their way back to the MAYFLOWER and told the impatient passengers that there was a chance of their being able to leave the ship and to start on the task of building their new homes.

On 15 December 1620 the anchor was weighed and they sailed into the bay. Next day, the first party landed to examine the coast more closely and to try to find the right site for their village. They saw with joy that the bay was full of fish, but the unfortunate thing was that they had forgotten to bring nets and they found, later, that their hooks were too large. As winter continued they lived to regret this as they grew shorter and shorter of food.

The landing party found several brooks running down into the bay; they saw that the soil was black and rich and that there was an abundance of trees both for timber and fruit—pines, walnut, beech, ash, birch and holly; cherry, plum and wild *vines*. There were herbs growing freely—*yarrow*, *sorrel*, *liverwort*, watercress and what looked like leeks and onions. They found, too, that there were sand and gravel, and clay which proved excellent for pot-making and as a substitute for soap.

There was some discussion as to where the village should be built. Some thought they should live on the island in the bay for security. This idea, however, was not

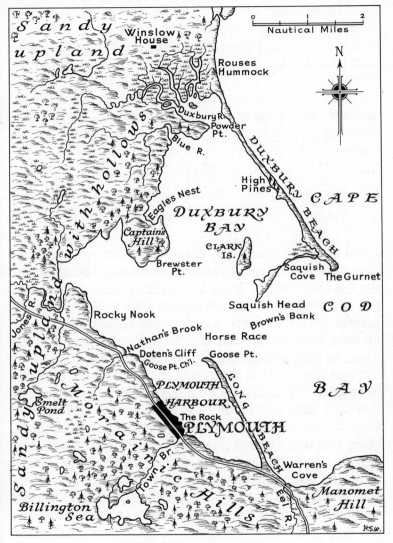

The site of the first landing

adopted, as none of the land was cleared and it was doubtful if there would be enough water. Instead they decided to settle on the high ground facing the harbour. There was land there already cleared of timber. They discovered later that this clearing had been made some years before by Indians who had all since died from an *epidemic*. At the bottom of the hill was a brook and there were several springs. On the highest point they decided

> 'to make a platform and plant our *ordnance* which will command all round about'

As you can see, they still feared an attack by Indians although, as yet, they had seen none around the bay.

> 'What people inhabit here we yet know not for as yet we have seen none.'

All was not plain sailing. It was midwinter, after all, and the next two or three days were stormy and wet and it was impossible to work. On 23 December a party went ashore to cut trees down to start building. This work went on for several days and there were several Indian alarms. No Indians were to be seen and I think, perhaps, that the Pilgrims were so expecting to be attacked that maybe they thought the howls of animals in the woods were the cries of savages. On Christmas Day they began to build the first house. It was to be mainly a storehouse where they could keep tools and put the muskets, powder, shot, clothing, shoes and other things they had brought with them. The way they built this and, later, their cottages, is interesting. They did not build log cabins. This is a widely held belief that is completely wrong. They built as they had learned to do in England. They chopped down trees, as wood was the only building material immediately handy but these tree trunks were sawn into planks. The logs were first squared with an *adze* and then laid over a saw-pit. This was a hole perhaps six or seven feet deep. Two men were needed. One was at the bottom of the pit and one at the top and they used a long two-handled saw vertically. It was a very effective way of cutting through the length of a tree trunk but it must have been very tiring, and extremely uncomfortable for the man at the bottom as all the sawdust fell on him. This was the traditional way of cutting planks in England and had been for hundreds of years.

These planks were mostly pine; for the framework of the cottage they used oak-tree beams which were again roughly squared. Once the frame was up, the planks were fastened on to it with wooden pins called 'tree nails' or 'trennels'. Making these pins was probably the work of the children. Holes had to be bored through the planks and into the beams and then they were pegged together. This, too, was typical English building practice. At one end was the chimney. This was made of wood but it was daubed with clay to try to prevent it catching fire. Once the frame and planks were up the roof was thatched with bulrushes

A model of an early Pilgrim cottage

and the first part of the job was done. They were not content, however, with this rather rough carpentry. Later the walls were covered inside with split cedar logs. They split the cedar with a great hammer they called a beetle and iron wedges. These thin pieces of cedar, fastened on with nails they had brought with them, made the inside much less bare. Each of the cottages had one room downstairs and a loft above reached by a ladder. The custom was, once the wood was ready cut, for all the men to have a 'house raising' which meant that the actual building could perhaps be done in a day. This custom lasted hundreds of years in America where it became the custom for all the neighbours to come round to 'raise' a house or barn and afterwards have a feast and a party to celebrate.

These were the first cottages. They were put up in a hurry in winter. All the Pilgrims tried to do was get some kind of shelter, so the buildings were very rough. When they had settled down they began to build better houses. There is a description of these houses of ten years later, on page 57. It will show you that they were good craftsmen and did not scorn comfort. I wonder if we should have been as clever.

Of course all these cottages were not built at once. They had to think of safety from the Indians and of planting crops so that they would not starve in the coming year. With so much to do, it was difficult to think which tasks were the most important to do first. What would you have started with?

They decided that they must think of shelter first. So, while some cut timber, others laid out the sites for the houses in a neat village street. First they counted the number of families—there were nineteen. Each unmarried man had to join a family and so reduce the number of separate cottages. Until the homes could be erected stakes marked each site. The boys and girls were sent out to gather reeds for thatching and others of the men kept watch for Indians. Everyone was busy because they all knew that if they did not get things going they would assuredly die.

There were continual little scares and excitements. On 3 January they saw smoke from what they assumed to be Indian fires and again on the 4th. Miles Standish and one or two others went out, armed, to find out if there were any enemies near but found nothing but some tumbledown old huts. They did, however, shoot an eagle and reported that the meat was excellent—just like mutton. On 12 January four men went out to cut thatch. They separated but, at the end of the day, two were missing. The two left searched for their missing companions but could not find them and returned to the village fearing them dead or captured. Apparently, so it turned out later, the lost pair, Goodman and Brown, had wandered farther than the others. They had their dogs with them—a mastiff and a spaniel. While they were cutting reeds the two dogs darted off in pursuit of a deer. Food was scarce in the settlement and it was a change from work; the two men went after them. Soon they were lost. Night fell; it was snowing and the only weapons they had were their sickles. Suddenly they heard what they thought were lions roaring. The only thing they could think of was to climb a tree if the fierce beasts approached. They found a tree that looked easy to climb and walked up and down all night around it. Next day they climbed a hill, saw the bay and managed to get back to their fellows. They were in a very sad state. Apart from being frightened almost to death, the exposure to the bitter weather had given them frost-bitten feet. There had been a great search for them and so everyone was very relieved when they turned up safely. Poor John Goodman seems to have been very unlucky. A few days later he had hobbled out to try out his poor feet, again with his spaniel, when two wolves came out of the trees and chased his dog. It ran between his legs for safety. Being unarmed, he threw a stick at the wolves who moved away a short distance but then, as he said when describing the scene later,

'they both sat on their tails grinning . . . a good while; and then went their way.'

On 16 January a man out hunting saw twelve Indians approaching. This was what the settlers had feared all along. Quickly the alarm was given; those who were working in the fields and the woods dashed back to the settlement, leaving their spades, axes and sickles behind and, seizing their muskets, prepared to defend themselves. The attack never came. Maybe the Indians had no intention of fighting; maybe they were put off by the thought that the

Pilgrims would fight back. All that happened was that the tools left in the woods vanished. Clearly, however, the Pilgrims could not risk a surprise attack and proper measures were taken for defence. Miles Standish, the only experienced soldier amongst them, was chosen to be captain. Guns were brought ashore from the MAYFLOWER and mounted on the platform at the top of the hill. We should not think these cannon very impressive but, for the time, they were quite powerful. There was a 'minion', $3\frac{1}{4}$-inch bore, a 'soller', $3\frac{1}{2}$-4-inch bore and a 'base', $1\frac{1}{4}$-inch bore. There can be no doubt that the settlers felt much more confident with these guns ashore and certainly the children would be delighted. I am quite certain that they would be a complete nuisance to the soldiers looking after the gun-platform. The master of the ship had, with great forethought, brought ashore with him when he brought the guns, a goose, a crane and a mallard. Food was always welcome.

Even though they felt more secure they always kept their muskets handy—in the fields, in the cottages and at service. They held their services every Sunday although they had no chapel. At first they would probably be in the storehouse; a little later they were in the fort they built on the hill. Not only had they no church, they also had no pastor. You will remember that John Robinson had stayed behind in Holland. The services were conducted by Elder, or Deacon, William Brewster until his death in 1643. There was, indeed, a parson sent out in 1624—the Rev. John Lyford—and the Pilgrims welcomed him and gave him a house. Very soon, however, they found that he was stirring up trouble and he was expelled. Deacon Brewster, therefore, continued to lead the services in the fort. The fort was used as a chapel until a proper one was built in the township in 1648.

Going back to the winter of 1620–21, the Pilgrims, always on the watch against the Indians, found life getting more and more difficult. It was not that the weather was desperately cold; if anything, for New England, it was quite mild but it was very wet. Can you imagine yourself working outside all day in the pouring rain and then coming home to a village whose street was just thick mud and houses that must have been damp and were certainly over-crowded with everyone living in one small room? It is no wonder that these conditions weakened everyone and, particularly, the very old and the very young. In addition many people were suffering from pneumonia and from typhus brought on by the dirty conditions. Food was fairly plentiful, though monotonous. There was corn bread, there was shellfish for the gathering, but no fish for, as we have seen, their hooks were too big and they had brought no nets, and there was wild fowl—duck, geese and turkey. The Pilgrims seem to have been very good shots with their muskets. Later on, on a visit to an Indian chief, a small party of them earned the gratitude of a band of Indians by shooting eighty crows that were destroying their crops. As a result of the 'Great Sickness', as it later became known, about half the original settlers died. When they were buried the survivors dared not mark their graves in case the Indians should see how weak they had become.

The first sign of relief came in the early part of March. For 3 March there is, in Bradford's Journal, an entry telling us that a warm south wind was blowing and that the birds were singing. There was also a surprise in March. Quite unexpectedly an Indian was seen walking, quite alone, down the village street between the cottages. This was startling enough: what was, to the settlers, almost incredible, was that he greeted them in English. He told them that he was a 'Sagamore' (or chief) and that he had

48

learned English from the fishermen who had
been coming across to the American coast a
little farther south for many years. The
settlers flocked round him. This was, perhaps, their great chance to get into contact
with the Indians and, maybe, make friends
with them. He was naked except for a '*breech-
clout*', was a straight, tall man with black hair
and carried a bow and two arrows. The Pilgrims took him and fed him with biscuits,
butter, cheese and brandy. In return he
answered their eager questions. He told them that the
place they had come to call 'New Plymouth' was known to
the Indians as 'Patuxet' and that, as we already know, all
the inhabitants had died. To the settlers' secret alarm the
Indian, who told them that his name was Samoset,
decided to stay the night. They lodged him in Stephen
Hopkins' cottage—and watched him. Next day he went
away; back, as he said, to Masasoit, the great chief in the
district. He told them that Masasoit was friendly but that
to the north there was another tribe, the Nausites, who
were very *hostile* to the English because, earlier, an English
captain had carried off some of their tribe as slaves.

Next day he came back bringing five more Indians with
him. The Journal tells us that they all wore long leggings
and, a point worthy of note in those bearded days, they had
no hair on their faces. Some also had their faces painted
black from forehead to chin. To show their friendliness
they brought with them the tools which they had
stolen in January. The five new ones soon left but
Samoset stayed on. It looked as though he had adopted the
Pilgrims and was showing them off to his friends—and at
the same time feeling very important as the one man who
could speak English and was not afraid of them. Quite

certainly, though the colonists feared the Indians, the Indians feared the white strangers even more. This time Samoset received more presents—a hat, a pair of stockings and a pair of shoes, a suit and a piece of cloth to tie around his waist.

On 19 March we have a short but very meaningful entry in the Journal:

'We dug and sowed garden seeds'—the ones they had brought with them—peas and beans in particular.

A day or two later Samoset, who had left after receiving his presents, came back with another Indian named Squanto who also spoke English. Squanto was the only surviving member of the tribe which had been wiped out by the epidemic. He had lived because he had been carried off as a slave and had actually been to England. They brought the news that Masasoit was near by and wished to visit them. This news made the Pilgrims both pleased and uneasy. They wished to be friendly with him yet they dare not, feeble as they were, allow him and his warriors into the village.

The decision as to what to do was the responsibility of the Governor and the freemen. This body of men governed the Colony. The Pilgrims were not foolish men. Even before they landed they had realized that even such a small settlement needed some kind of government if it was to flourish. They had, therefore, drawn up a *document* called the 'Mayflower Compact'. This was signed by the forty-one males on board. They agreed:

'That when they came on shore they would use their own liberty, for none had power to command them.' (By this they meant that they could form whatever kind of government they wished because although they were supposed to have landed in Virginia they had not really done so and so earlier decisions in England did not apply.) You can see a *facsimile* of the agreement on page 66 but here are some extracts:

'In the name of God, Amen. We whose names are underwritten, the loyall subjects of our dread soveraigne Lord, King James . . . having undertaken a voyage to plant ye first colonie in ye northerne parts of Virginia do . . . combine ourselves together into a civil *body politick* for our better ordering and preservation . . . to enact . . . such just and equal lawes, ordinances, acts, constitutions and offices from time to time as shall be thought most *meete* . . . A.D. 1620.'

The government as laid down provided for a Governor (and later Assistants) to be elected annually by the freemen of the colony. The first freemen were the forty-one *signatories* to the Compact. Each year more were admitted. Each candidate had to be 21 years old or more and have a good reputation. If accepted, the new freeman was admitted at a formal meeting or 'Court'. Each year all the freemen met in assembly and sat with the Governor and his assistants to pass laws. All this, of course, developed as

The Pilgrims welcome the Indians

51

the needs of the new Colony made it necessary. At the time of the Indians' visit the Governor, John Carver, decided that they could not admit all the warriors and so they sent Edward Winslow, dressed in a full suit of armour and girt with his sword, across the Town Brook, which marked the edge of the settlement, to greet the king and to present him with knives, a copper chain containing a jewel, an ear-ring, a pot of brandy and some buttered ships'-biscuits. Winslow stayed as a *hostage* while Masasoit and twenty braves crossed the brook. They were met by Captain Standish and six men who fired a salute. The Indians were taken to a cottage and seated on a green rug to await the Governor.

They were a rare sight. The chief's face was painted red and his followers had decorated themselves as the fancy took them. Some had painted black stripes on themselves, some red, some yellow and some, obviously more artistic, white stripes with crosses. To try to impress the Indians the Pilgrims put on as much of a show as they could. When the Governor came he was escorted by a bodyguard playing drums and trumpets. It must have been a wonderful scene: a group of soberly dressed, hardy farmers marching through a huddle of *unkempt* cabins down a muddy path to the accompaniment of martial music to confer with a group of wildly painted half-naked savages. Despite the strangeness of the sight, however, both sides were anxious for peace and it was made. They agreed not only not to attack each other but, also, to help each other. Terms of trade were also settled.

It is not quite true to say that all the colonists were earnest and hardworking. There was at least one family that seemed continually to be in trouble or making a nuisance of itself. We find that in March, for example, one John Billington was brought before the Governor and Freemen and charged with making rude remarks about the Captain—presumably Miles Standish. It is worthy of notice that the Pilgrims were no more *tolerant* of people who did not fit in than were the authorities in England from whom they had fled. Billington was found guilty and was sentenced to be *trussed* up by the neck and heels for twenty-four hours. He begged their pardon, however, and was released. Later, in August, John Billington junior was lost. The whole day's work was upset while searches were made everywhere for the boy but he could not be found. The Indians brought the news that he had been seen with the Nausite Indians and a party had to be sent to fetch him home.

In April two great events took place. First the MAY-FLOWER finally sailed for England. So long as the ship was there the colonists felt that there was always a place of safety. Now they were alone. Secondly Governor Carver died and was replaced by Governor Bradford to whose Journal we owe so much.

In June there was another strange event which maybe changes our opinion of the Pilgrims a little. Obviously some were wealthier than others. Mr Stephen Hopkins, we find, had two servants—Edward Doty and Edward Leister. Equally obviously, these servants were not *devout Puritans* for we find them arrested for fighting a *duel* with swords and daggers. Both were wounded but were, nevertheless, sentenced to be trussed up without food for twenty-four hours. Their master, however, begged for their release and, as they were both in pain from their wounds, it was agreed to.

In June the colonists decided to send a small party to pay a *formal* visit to Masasoit and his tribe. The leaders were Stephen Hopkins and Edward Winslow. They took with them a red cotton cloak with lace for the chief. Their purpose, in addition, was to tell the chief that, while they were delighted to see him at the settlement, they had, at this time, insufficient food to feed him and his followers. For three days they tramped through the heat to find his camp. When they finally reached the chief he agreed to their requests, gave them tobacco, and talked, and talked. You will probably know that tobacco was one of the native plants the colonists found growing in America and that they learnt from the Indians how to smoke it. The travellers were both hungry and tired but no food appeared and the chief went on talking. At last, supperless, they went to bed in a tent which they shared with the chief and his family and two of his followers. Next day one of the braves shot two fishes with an arrow. These were shared among everyone. This was all the travellers had to eat in seventy-two hours. Winslow reported on their return:

> 'with bad lodging, the savages' barbarous singing (for they like to sing themselves to sleep), *lice* and fleas within doors and mosquitoes without, we could hardly sleep at all.'

It was not long before their friendship with Masasoit was put to the test. News reached the colonists that a lesser chief, Corbitant, was plotting against Masasoit and had driven him from his village. They had decided to support their friend when they heard that two friendly Indians, Squanto and Hobbamoch, who had gone to see Masasoit, had been captured by Corbitant. The Pilgrims, therefore, got together an armed party of ten under Captain Standish and sent them off to deal with Corbitant. When they got near the Indian encampment they hid, thinking that a night attack would be both more effective and safer, for, after all, there were only ten of them. They did not know what they might find, for Hobbamoch, who had escaped, reported that Squanto had been killed by

Corbitant. In the dark they had a quick meal and then crept forward and surrounded Corbitant's tent. When they burst in everyone was terrified. They all swore that Corbitant had gone and that Squanto was still alive. The Pilgrims told them that they were going to harm no one; that Corbitant was the only one they wanted. This sudden attack by these grim-faced strangers so frightened Corbitant's fellow-plotters that they too fled. The *conspiracy* collapsed and Masasoit recovered his position with even friendlier feelings towards the colonists.

Soon, after hard work, suffering, death and danger, the Pilgrims were approaching the end of their first year in America. Many had died, but those who still lived had triumphed over the worst dangers. Friendly relations had been established with the Indians, land had been cleared, crops sown and harvested.

The first Thanksgiving

55

'We have built seven dwelling houses, four for the use of the plantation and prepared for many others. We have sowed twenty acres of Indian corn and six acres of barley and pease.'

They were thankful and they celebrated the First Thanksgiving

The Colony after the First Year

Houses

After the difficulties of the first year or two the Pilgrims began to find life a little easier so they turned to making their houses more comfortable. By 1630 the normal house, still of oak and pine, was built around a great central brick chimney. The outer wooden planks were never painted but were allowed to weather naturally to a dark grey or brown. To avoid the risk of fire, the roof was, by law, no longer thatched. There were usually two ground-floor rooms—a parlour (living-room, dining-room, spare bedroom) and a kitchen. Each room had a great open fireplace. On the first floor, up a winding staircase, were two bedrooms and over them a loft. The walls of the rooms inside were sheathed with split cedar and the space between the two layers was packed with dried grass which helped to keep out the cold.

The windows, which had been of oiled paper, were now filled with small diamond-shaped pieces of glass held together by strips of lead. Over the windows were heavy wool curtains. The floors were made of wide pine planks that were scoured white with beach sand. Imagine scrubbing floors with sand rather than soap! There were no rugs or carpets. Each home had, by it, a barn and sheds. Here were kept the cattle, poultry, pigs, hay, corn and other crops and, of course, the various tools.

There was, of course, no plumbing in the house. The lavatory, would be at the bottom of the garden and the water supply came from a well.

The furnishings, like the house, were home-made. Chairs were rare—just as they were in England—and most people sat on stools or benches. The beds were often rough imitations of the much more elaborate *four-posters* they had seen in England. A really precious possession was a mattress stuffed with goose-feathers. Most people had to use odds and ends of wool or cloth. They had plenty of blankets, pillows and pillowcases which they called 'pillowbeers'.

On the table most dishes were wooden, though some were of *pewter*. Similarly, spoons were wood or pewter, though occasionally there would be an iron toasting fork. Forks were not used for eating. There were no drinking glasses or bottles. Containers for liquids were made of leather or pewter. Every good housewife had two wooden tubs. One was for the laundry. The New Englanders called washing clothes 'bucking'—perhaps this comes from the slapping of the clothes with wooden paddles. The other tub was for salting meat for the winter.

Food

For breakfast most people had 'hasty pudding'. This was a kind of porridge made with cornflour. It was sometimes called 'corn meal mush'. It was eaten with milk and *molasses*.

Dinner was eaten from eleven to twelve. Frequently hasty pudding was served again with the addition of fresh or salt fish, or beef, or pork or mutton.

One favourite dish was 'succotash' which was made of

Two pounds of steak.
One boiled chicken.
Two cups of peas.
Three pints of corn.
Four potatoes.

58

In addition, there were wild fruits in their seasons—straw-berries, blueberries, raspberries and blackberries. For vegetables they had peas, turnips, onions, squash and pumpkins. Although modern Americans eat pumpkin pie at Thanksgiving, the original settlers used it to make a sauce. One point—there were *no* cranberries.

Dress

The Pilgrims did not spend all their time dressed in black suits, white collars and high hats. Possibly they had such clothes for best but normally the men wore grey, brown or blue long-sleeved linen shirts, a brown leather jacket called a jerkin, woollen or leather breeches, knitted stock-ings and either shoes or high boots. On the top they wore a cloak and a wool stocking-cap.

The women wore long, brightly-coloured dresses.

Behaviour

They were Puritans and so always behaved soberly. The Sabbath was always kept strictly from sunset on Saturday to sunset on Sunday. No work was done during these twenty-four hours and there were, of course, no games or amusements. There was Divine Worship morning and afternoon. Everybody was expected to attend and to obey the teaching of the Church. If they could not do this they were exiled from the Colony.

There was very little crime indeed. There were only five murders in the whole history of the Colony. One, the first, took place in 1630. John Billington shot and killed another man. He was tried by the Governor, William Bradford and his assistants in the Court of Freemen, and found guilty. Bradford was doubtful if he could order him to be hanged without first obtaining approval from London. He asked the governor of a neighbouring colony for advice and was told to hang him and forget about it. So Billington was hanged. The colonists, however, were well in advance of their time. They never used torture or burned witches. Apart from hangings, the worst punishment was exile.

Defence

In 1622 danger appeared from the Nanganset Indians. The Indians sent the Pilgrims a snakeskin containing a bundle of arrows. This was almost a declaration of war. The Pilgrims, never ones to refuse a challenge, sent the snakeskin back filled with bullets. Nevertheless, though the attack never came, they began to look to their defences.

'But this made them more carefully to looke to themselves, so as they agreed to inclose their dwellings with a good strong *pale*, and made flankers in convenient places, with gates to shute, which were every night locked and a watch kept, and where need required there was also *warding* in ye day time. And ye Company was by ye captaine and ye Governor's advice, devided into 4 squadrons, and everyone had ther quarter appoynted them, unto which they were to *repaire* upon any sudden alarme. And if ther should be any crie of fire, a company were appointed for a guard with muskets, whilst others quenchet ye same to prevent Indian treachoury. This was accomplished very cherfully and ye toune *impayled* round by ye beginning of March, in which every family had a pretty garden plot secured.'

The seal of the colony

60

Some Pilgrims

John Robinson

'His name stood, and shall stand, first in the history of the Pilgrims and in the history of the United States.'

This is the opinion of a twentieth-century historian: it is the same as that held by the Pilgrims themselves, even though Robinson was one who stayed behind in Holland.

Like the other Pilgrims he came from the countryside around Scrooby. He was born in Sturton-le-Steeple, a little town a few miles to the east of Scrooby. His father owned a farm there and was quite prosperous. Robinson grew up surrounded by those devout men who suffered so much and, naturally, was very much affected by their ideas.

When he was 17 he went to Corpus Christi College at the University of Cambridge. In 1595 he became a Bachelor of Arts and in 1599 a Master of Arts. While there, he became a priest in the Church of England, but was soon forced to give up his work because of his Puritan ideas. He joined the people of Scrooby in their attempts to reach Holland.

When the party finally settled in Leyden he became their greatly beloved pastor. He was admired by the Dutch and loved by his flock. He supported the move to America but was unable to go with them.

Edward Winslow, one of the leaders, wrote an account of Robinson's last message and prayer to his friends. It was truer than he knew. He said that

'we were now ere long to part asunder: and the Lord knoweth whether ever he should live to see our faces again'.

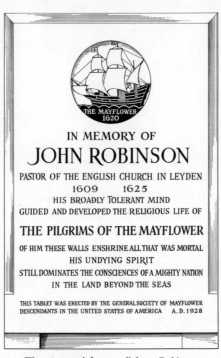

IN MEMORY OF

JOHN ROBINSON

PASTOR OF THE ENGLISH CHURCH IN LEYDEN

1609   1625

HIS BROADLY TOLERANT MIND

GUIDED AND DEVELOPED THE RELIGIOUS LIFE OF

THE PILGRIMS OF THE MAYFLOWER

OF HIM THESE WALLS ENSHRINE ALL THAT WAS MORTAL

HIS UNDYING SPIRIT

STILL DOMINATES THE CONSCIENCES OF A MIGHTY NATION

IN THE LAND BEYOND THE SEAS

THIS TABLET WAS ERECTED BY THE GENERAL SOCIETY OF MAYFLOWER
DESCENDANTS IN THE UNITED STATES OF AMERICA   A.D. 1928

The   memorial   to   John   Robinson

He died on 1 March 1625.

Roger White reported to New Plymouth:

'He fell sicke ye 22 of Feb. and departed this life ye 1 of March. He had a continuous inward *ague,* but free from infection, so all his friends came freely to him. And if either prayers, tears or means would have saved his life, he had not gone hence. But he, having faithfully finished his course and performed his worke which ye had appointed him here to do, he now resteth with ye Lorde in eternall hapiness.'

William Brewster

Next to Robinson stands William Brewster. He too was at Cambridge University and, as we have seen, was an important man in Scrooby. He was one of the leading Separatists and a strong supporter of the move to Holland.

He found life in Leyden hard because, unlike most of the Pilgrims, he had no skill as a craftsman and work was hard to find. For a time he earned his living by teaching English to students at the University. In 1617, however, he became associated with what has since become known as the Pilgrim Press. This was a small printing firm which was partly concerned in producing books for sale, but mainly in printing Puritan *pamphlets* and books for the *brethren* in England. The English printers were forbidden to touch them. These books were sent secretly to England and circulated widely there to the fury of King James. The books carried no printer's name and the English government moved heaven and earth to find out where they came from. At last it discovered the press in Leyden and demanded that Brewster, and his partner Brewer, be handed over. The Dutch were most unwilling to do this and Brewster was allowed to vanish. There is no more trace of him as 'Brewster' on this side of the Atlantic. His name appears on no more documents nor is it to be found on the MAYFLOWER list. There was, however, a passenger called Williamson who appeared from nowhere. Possibly this was Brewster since it was the Dutch custom to call people by their fathers' Christian names. For example, 'Jonothan Brewster' is called in the Dutch records 'Jonothan Willemsz' (i.e., son of William) and as the elder Brewster's father was also called William, it was an appropriate disguise.

In New England Brewster became an elder of the Church and took a full part in all the adventures and hardships. He lived there about twenty-four years and died about the age of eighty.

William Bradford

Bradford was born in Austerfield in Yorkshire in 1590. At an early age he became a great student of the Bible and an enthusiastic Puritan. He attended the services at Brewster's home in Scrooby and joined the group in its move to Holland. In Leyden he followed the trade of a weaver. In 1617 he was one of the leaders and did much to organize the voyage to America.

He took part in the boat expeditions from Cape Cod and is supposed to have been the first man to land on Plymouth Rock on the site of the future village. When he returned from this expedition he found that his wife, Dorothy, had fallen over the side of the MAYFLOWER and had drowned.

In 1621, after the death of Governor Carver, Bradford was chosen Governor. He held this office for thirty-three years.

He guided the colony through its difficult early years and endeared himself to all students of history by writing a most detailed journal of these years. Most of the facts in this book come from this diary.

He died in 1657 at the age of 67.

Miles Standish

Standish was born in Lancashire about 1584. In his early life he was a professional soldier fighting for Holland against Spain. Here, probably, he met the Pilgrims and sailed with them to America. He was, probably, the only soldier and so was appointed the Captain. He was responsible for the defence of the colony and, with his army of some twelve men, succeeded admirably. He was for a time assistant-governor but never became a member of the Pilgrim Church. He died in 1656.

Edward Winslow

Winslow was born in Droitwich in 1595 and was brought up a Puritan. In 1517 he joined the Pilgrims in Leyden and became a member of John Robinson's Church. He sailed with them in the MAYFLOWER. His wife, Elizabeth, died soon after their arrival in New Plymouth. Later he married Susannah White. This was the first marriage in New England. He was always one of the leading members of the group and, in 1644, was Governor. He returned to England several times. The drawing below is a copy of his portrait which hangs in the gallery of the Pilgrim Society at Plymouth, Massachusetts. It is supposed to be the only genuine likeness of any of the MAYFLOWER Pilgrims.

Edward Winslow—the only genuine portrait of a pilgrim

THE MAYFLOWER COMPACT

IN yᵉ name of God Amen. We whofe names are vnder-writen, the loyall subjects of our dread foueraigne Lord King James, by yᵉ grace of God, of Great Britaine, Franc, & Ireland, king, defender of yᵉ faith, etc. Haueing vndertaken, for yᵉ glorie of God, and aduancemente of yᵉ Christian faith and honour of our king & countrie, a voyage to plant yᵉ first colonie in yᵉ Northerne parts of Virginia, doe by thefe prefents solemnly & mutualy in yᵉ prefence of God, and one of another, couenant & combine our felves togeather into a ciuill body politick, for our better ordering & preferuation & furtherance of yᵉ ends aforefaid; and by vertue hearof to enacte, constitute, and frame fuch just & equall lawes, ordinances, acts, constitutions, & offices, from time to time, as fhall be thought most meete and conuenient for yᵉ generall good of yᵉ Colonie: vnto which we promife all due submiffion and obedience. In witnes wherof we haue hereunder subfcribed our names at Cap-Codd yᵉ .11. of Nouember, in yᵉ year of yᵉ raigné of our soueraigne Lord King James of England, France, & Ireland yᵉ eighteenth, and of Scotland yᵉ fiftie fourth. Anᵒ: dom: 1620.

John Carter
William Bradford
Edu'ard Winflow
William Breufter
Ifaac Allerton
Myles Standifh
John Alden
John Turner
Francis Eaton
James Chilton
John Crackfton
John Billington
Mofes Fletcher
John Goodman

Samuel Fuller
Chriftopher Martin
William Mullins
William White
Richard Warren
John Howland
Stephen Hopkins
Degory Prieft
Thomas Williams
Gilbert Winflow
Edmund Margefon
Peter Brown
Richard Britteridge
George Soule

Edward Tilley
John Tilley
Francis Cooke
Thomas Rogers
Thomas Tinker
John Ridgdale
Edward Fuller
Richard Clark
Richard Gardiner
John Allerton
Thomas Englifh
Edward Doty
Edward Leifter

The ' Mayflower' Compact

John Carver, Katherine his wife, Desire Minter, and two man-servants, John Howland, Roger Wilder; William Latham a boy, a maidservant and a child Jasper More.   8

William Brewster, Mary his wife, two sons Love and Wrestling; a boy Richard More, and another brother   6

Edward Winslow, Elizabeth his wife. Two men-servants, George Soule and Elias Story, and a little girl Ellen, sister of Richard More.   5

William Bradford and Dorothy his wife.   2

Isaac Allerton, Mary his wife, and three children, Bartholomew, Remember and Mary, and a servant John Hooke.   6

Samuel Fuller and his servant William Button.   2

John Crackston and his son.   2

Captain Miles Standish and Rose his wife.   2

Christopher Martin, his wife and two servants.   4

William Mullins, his wife and two children, Joseph and Priscilla, and one servant.   5

William White, his wife Susanna, one son Resolved and one born on ship, Peregrine, and two servants.   6

Stephen Hopkins, Elizabeth his wife, four children, Giles, Constanta, Damaris and Oceanus (born at sea), and two servants.   8

Richard Warren.   1

John Billington, Ellen his wife and two sons, John and Francis.   4

Edward Tilley, his wife and two children Henry and Humility.   4

John Tilley, his wife and daughter. 3

Francis Cooke and his son John. 2

Thomas Rogers and Joseph his son. 2

Thomas Timber, his wife and son. 3

John Rigsdale and Alice his wife. 2

James Chilton, his wife and daughter Mary. 3

Edward Fuller, his wife and Samuel his son. 3

John Turner and two sons. 3

Francis Eaton, Sarah his wife and Samuel his son. 3

Moses Fletcher, John Goodman, Thomas Williams, Diggory Priest, Edmund Margesson, Peter Browne, Richard Brittenidge, Richard Clarke, Richard Gardiner, Gilbert Winslow. 10

John Alden, hired as a cooper in Southampton—decided to stay in New England. 1

John Allerton and Thomas English, hired as the master of the shallop and as a seaman. They died in New England before the ship returned.

Total: 100

Records

One died at sea.

Fifty-one died in first year.

One executed for murder.

1679—Twelve original settlers alive.

1690—Three alive.

1694—Two alive.

1699—Mary (Allerton) Cushman, born 1616, died 1699. The last survivor.

'Mayflower II'

On 4 July, American Independence Day, 1955, work on MAYFLOWER II began in the shipyard of Stuart Upham of Brixham in Devon. Douglas Kenelm Winslow, a descendant of Edward Winslow, whose portrait you have seen, laid the keel on 28 July.

So began for Warwick Charlton a period of hectic hard work. He had, at the end of the war, had a vision of the re-creation of the voyage of the pilgrims to cement the friendship between Britain and America. He had gained support for his project in both countries—support both financial and technical. Many people gave him money; business firms offered him sails and ropes and all kinds of things that would be necessary on the voyage. He was quite determined that the ship itself should be built and paid for by Britain but he gladly accepted the offer of a set of ship's plans from an American, a Mr. Baker, which were based on the latest research on the MAYFLOWER. Similarly, since the ship was to be presented to the American people, he was delighted to receive the enthusiastic co-operation of 'Plimouth Plantation Incorporated', a body of private citizens who were rebuilding the original Pilgrim Settlement in Plymouth, Massachussets. They promised to provide a permanent home for the ship.

Building the Ship

Stuart Upham's firm was an old-established one that had specialised in the building of wooden ships. But, in addition to their long acquaintance with the methods, the members of the firm had to do a lot of research to find out how the old ships were built and what tools were used. Here are some of the old tools used, as described by Charlton:

'The adze, the first tool of the shipwright's tool chest; the axe, for the rough trimming of logs; the gimbletts for boring holes before brace-and-bit were invented, gauges for scribing, augers for long boring to ensure watertightness . . . mawls for driving bolts . . .'

Charlton was quite determined that, as far as possible, the second MAYFLOWER should not only look like the first one but be made by the same methods.

For example, the planking was fastened to the frame by the treenails we came across earlier when the pilgrims were building their houses. These, twenty inches long, were made out of some 130-year-old Devon cider casks. The wood had to be seasoned because unseasoned timber would shrink and allow water in.

The timber for the frame caused a lot of trouble. The countryside had to be scoured for oak trees that were not only big but were also growing in the particular curve needed for a particular beam. Word spread around and news of trees began to come in. Some weighed up to ten tons and were nearly 200 years old. The tree used for the main stem was huge. It was six feet in circumference and contained 116 cubic feet of solid oak.

All manner of other material had to be obtained, made or found but, at last, in a drenching rain-storm on 22 September, MAYFLOWER II was launched with full seventeenth-century ceremony.

The Vicar of Brixham began the Service of Dedication at the bow of the ship with the hymn

O God of Jacob, by whose hand,
Thy people still are fed . . .

and continued with a prayer of Sir Francis Drake; then
followed the 23rd Psalm and a prayer by Abraham Lin-
coln was added.

All this time the storm was raging and there were peals
of thunder.

The ship was launched by a young American, Reis
Leming. The christening cup was passed around the
shipwrights until it returned to Reis. Then in the bows,
he drained the cup and, according to old custom, cast it
into the sea with the words

'I name thee—MAYFLOWER.'

Contrary to custom a swimmer recovered the cup and
presented it to Reis.

The Sailing

The crew was picked, the fitting-out was completed, the cargo was packed and, on 20 April the MAYFLOWER II set sail from Plymouth on a voyage that was to last until 12 June. Warwick Charlton kept a daily journal. Here are some extracts.

Second Day, Sunday, 21 April: Easter Sunday.

'... the first person I saw at the wheel on this, our first real day at sea, was John Winslow.... He has begun to grow a beard, but only down one side of his face to win a wager struck with the other seamen that he will arrive in America half clean-shaven, half-bearded.'

Eighth Day, Saturday, 27 April

'By noon today we will have been at sea for a week and we have made about eight hundred miles ... but we have over five thousand more before we make our landfall at Plymouth.'

Forty-seventh Day, Thursday, 6 June.

'There was a squall coming up astern and I went up on the poop to try to see through glasses what was happening to the destroyers. Suddenly they began to move toward us ... until they passed in line abreast ... I had the honour of dipping the Red Duster to return the salute ... each warship making a personal tribute to the little wooden ship sailing northwest through grey sheets of rain to the New England of the Pilgrim Fathers.'

Forty-eighth Day, Friday, 7 June.

' ... at eleven o'clock I was woken by the motion of the ship as she pitched and rolled heavily. I ran out ... to find we were caught in a wind of gale force and a confused and angry sea ... the wind was strong enough to snap the topmast ...'

Fifty-second Day, Monday, 10 June: Whit Monday.

'Becalmed—our first visitor was a fishing vessel; she came alongside and gave us six enormous lobsters. Later in the morning we sighted the periscope of a submarine ...'

Fifty-fifth Day, Thursday, 13 June 1957.

' . . . set all sail and an east wind took us across Cape Cod Bay . . . a gay armada of several hundred boats was attracted to us . . . whistles, sirens, fog-horns, rattles, cannon . . . for the last time the crew, to a great cheer, ran up the rigging to the yardarms, and, in the billowing sleeves, woollen caps and buckled shoes of their seventeenth-century costume, took in all sail.'

'A few minutes before twelve o'clock we made fast at the buoy and swung slowly around in the harbour.

'After about an hour a cannon boomed, and, at its signal, the shallop which had been built by Plimouth Plantation for the occasion, sped out from the shore to meet us. I went with Alan and the first landing party to the ramp at the side of Plymouth Rock.'

THINGS TO DO

1. Draw a picture of the First Thanksgiving. Try to find out more from books and newspapers or films about how Americans celebrate Thanksgiving today.

2. Do you think that people should be punished for their beliefs? You could discuss this in class.

2a. Discuss the differences between the way the Puritans of Scrooby spent Sunday (see page 9) and the way we spend it.

3. Draw a large map to go on the class-room notice board showing the route of the Pilgrims from Scrooby to Leyden. Try to find out more details about Amsterdam and Leyden. You could write to the Dutch Tourist Office or, maybe, try to get pen-friends in Holland.

4. The Pilgrims earned their living by all kinds of trades in Leyden. What kinds of work would modern pilgrims do in similar circumstances? There are such refugees today, of course. Find out as much as you can about different reasons for refugees today.

5. Imagine you travelled in the *Mayflower*. Write an account of the voyage as you saw it.

6. Draw a large picture of the *Mayflower* for the class notice-board. Put by it drawings of the navigational instruments with notes on how they were used.

7. Do you think you would have liked to live in New England in those early days? Give your reasons for saying 'Yes' or 'No'.

8. Draw a large map of the early settlement. Put by it a map of New England today and notice the differences.

9. Try to make a model of the early settlement. Use a big drawing board. Make the hills and valleys of plasticine, clay or plaster. Make trees with pins or matchsticks with coloured pieces of sponge; the cabins can be made of cardboard or small pieces of wood stuck together.

10. Try to write a journal yourself, describing all the day-by-day events of one whole week during the first year at New Plymouth.

11. Write and act a scene in which the Indian chief Masasoit first meets the Governor, or paint a picture of the scene (see p. 52.)

12. Write a story about Red Indians and English settlers.

13. Draw up a list of the twelve most important rules for the government of New Plymouth which you would have made in the first year of settlement.

14. Look carefully at the memorial to John Robinson on p. 62. Find out who erected it and when. Why do you think they did this?

GLOSSARY

The most difficult words in the book are printed like *this*. This is a list of them with their meanings:

adze : an axe with the blade at right angles to the normal axe blade.

aft : towards the back of a ship.

ague : fever: makes the sick person shake as though shivering.

altar : communion table in church.

Anglican : belonging to the Church of England.

apothecary : old name for a chemist who sold medicines, etc.

archbishop : usually the head of the Church in a country (Anglican or Roman Catholic).

astrolabe : a navigation aid—measures the angle of the sun.

asunder : apart.

baize : coarse woollen cloth usually dyed one colour.

barricade : fence or other barrier to stop an attack.

base : very small cannon.

betwixt : between two other people, objects or places.

binnacle : box containing compass, etc.

bishop : church official working under an archbishop.

bitters : liquid into which a bitter herb has been mixed.

blackfish : small-toothed whale.

body politick : an old way of describing the citizens of a state or country.

bosun : short for boatswain—a sailor in charge of sails, anchors and ropes.

bowed : bent.

bowsprit : large pole sticking out from front of ship.

breech-clout : piece of cloth wound round the waist and between the legs.

brethren : brothers—meaning people who had similar opinions or beliefs.

burden : weight of cargo a ship could carry.

calibre : diameter of the hole in the barrel of the cannon.

chains : chains holding the anchors.

chaos : utter confusion.

charge : expense.

civil war : people of the same nation fighting each other.

cobbler : boot repairer or, perhaps, boot-maker.

compass : always points in the direction of the North Pole.

conspiracy : plot.

corn : Indian corn or maize—what your cornflakes are made from.

course : proper direction or route for the ship.

cranberry : bright red, rather acid berry.

crane : tall wading bird rather like a heron.

crucifix : the Cross carrying an image of Christ.

culverin : long cannon.

cutlass : short, heavy curving sword.

demi-cannon :
demi-culverin : } small cannon.

to denounce : to accuse someone or to inform against them.

despatches : messages—usually written.

devout : very religious.

document : paper containing some important writing.

doulfull : sad, sorrowful.

draper : either a maker or seller of cloth or both.

duel : fight between two people—usually with sword or pistol.

elders : senior members of a Presbyterian church who help the minister.

to emigrate : to leave one's native country to live in another.

emigrant : someone who emigrates.

epidemic : disease that has spread very widely among a lot of people.

to exercise : to carry out drill with swords and muskets.

exercise : religious service.

facsimile : exact copy or reproduction of something.

faggot : wood for burning on the fire—a log.

fathom : seven feet.

fervent : enthusiastic.

fo'c'sle : forecastle, or front part of ship.

foremast : mast nearest the front of ship.

fore-sail : largest sail attached to foremast.

fore-topsail : smaller sail above fore-sail.

formal : done in the proper way or in a regular way.

four-poster : bed with four posts which carry a frame with curtains which draw all round the bed.

fowling : hunting wild birds.

freemen : the original travellers on the *Mayflower* who signed the Compact.

glazed : looking as though they were covered with glass.

hatchway : opening in deck covered by a trapdoor.

hazard : risk, danger.

hostage : member of one side left in the power of the other side to make sure there is no treachery.

hostile : unfriendly, enemy.

impaled : fenced.

infested : full of; crowded with, usually unpleasant creatures.

interloper : stranger; someone who seems to have no right to be there.

landfall : first sight of land at the end of a voyage.

latitude : lines on a map marking the distance north or south of the Equator.

leadsman : sailor who finds the depth of the water with a lead-weighted line.

lice : insects that live in dirt and bite you.

liquor : drink—usually alcoholic.

liverwort : herb with liver-shaped leaves and small white, pink or blue flowers.

log and line : a way of measuring the speed of a ship.

Low Countries : Holland and Belgium.

lusty : sturdy, big and strong.

mainmast : largest mast on the ship; in the middle if there are three.

mainsail : principal sail.

main-topsail : smaller sail above the mainsail.

mallard : wild duck.

mariner : sailor.

Marsdiep : inland water in Holland.

meete : suitable.

minion : small cannon.

mizzen-mast : rear mast on a ship.

molasses : form of syrup used for sweetening; often taken from the maple tree.

molested : harmed or attacked.

multitude : crowd.

musket : gun carried by soldiers—fired a ball, not a bullet.

muzzle : mouth of a gun.

ordnance : guns.

pale : fence.

pamphlet : small paper-covered booklet.

pastor : minister of religion.

patriotic : loving one's own country.

pewter : metal used for cups and plates—mixture of iron and tin.

port : opening in a ship's side—usually small.

prairie : open grassland covering a large area.

prayer-book : printed form of church service.

Presbyterian : church governed by 'elders'.

pumpkin : large egg-shaped or round vegetable, like a marrow.

Puritan : man who likes a simple form of religion.

ransacked : plundered, robbed.

Reformation : the break-away from the Roman Catholic Church in the sixteenth century.

rendezvous : meeting-place.

to repaire : to go.

revered : greatly respected and beloved.

rifled : robbed.

saker : small cannon.

sand-glass : like an egg-timer; the sand falls from one compartmen to another in a certain time.

seams : joints between the planks of a ship.

shallop : light open boat for use on rivers; usually carried oars and a sail.

signatories : people who have signed a document.

sickle : curved, sharpened blade like a half-moon, used for reaping.

soller : another small cannon.

sorrel : herb with pleasant acid-tasting leaves.

sprit-sail : sail which goes across other sails diagonally.

squash : vegetable rather like a pumpkin.

stagnant : not flowing; foul from lack of movement.

steerage : place whence the ship was steered; the rear of the ship.

stern : rear of a ship.

surplice : white linen outer garment worn by Roman Catholic and Anglican priests in church—also by choristers.

synod : church council.

tacklings : jobs they had to do.

tiller : wooden bar attached to the rudder by which the rudder was moved.

tolerant : prepared to allow other people to have opinions differing from your own.

traitor : one who betrays his country or sovereign.

trussed : fastened up with a rope.

unkempt : untidy; rough-looking.

vassal : servant; one who has to obey a lord.

venison : meat of deer.

vestments : various special robes worn by some priests.

victuals : food.

vines : shrubs on which grapes grow.

warding : guarding.

whipstaff : device by which the helmsman could steer the ship from the top deck.

yarrow : strongly scented herb.

Zuider Zee : inlet of the North Sea running into Holland.